Soothe *the* Soul

One step,
one breath,
one moment
to the next.

Give yourself
the peace you've
been looking for.

Let the moment pause,
just here. Just now.

What do you feel?

Stretch your arms, your face, your neck

Make a cup of hot tea and enjoy the steam rising

Play a soft song with your eyes closed

Write down a few words in a journal

*Step outside for a short walk,
feel the solidness of the ground beneath you*

*Tuck yourself under a cozy blanket,
and take a few deep breaths*

AFFIRMATION
for nourishing your spirit

I GIVE MYSELF

WHAT I

DEEPLY NEED.

I FIND SPACE

TO GO SLOWLY,

AND TO

WELCOME JOY.

This is a beautiful and simple change of lifestyle. A lifestyle of letting go and living openhandedly, curled up in the sunlit warmth...

JULIE SARAH POWELL

What makes you smile?

_____

_____

_____

_____

_____

What lifts your spirits?

_____

_____

_____

_____

_____

What do you want most?

_____

_____

_____

_____

_____

Don't ask yourself
what the world needs,
ask yourself what
makes you come alive.
And then go and do
that. Because what the
world needs is people
who have come alive.

HOWARD WASHINGTON THURMAN

Be distracted, positively.

What healthy habits do you enjoy?

- ○ Listening to a podcast
- ○ Singing or dancing along to music
- ○ Reading quietly
- ○ Getting out and moving your body
- ○ Yoga or meditation
- ○ Watching an inspiring show
- ○ Painting, writing, or being creative
- ○ Helping others
- ○ Walking in nature
- ○ Connecting with loved ones
- ○ Going for a long drive
- ○ Buying yourself flowers
- ○ Unplugging for a set amount of time
- ○ Trying a new food, place, or experience

MEDITATION: *Attention*

Give yourself a few minutes to be completely aware. Use all of your senses to take in all that is around you, and all that is within. What is the color of the light? Where do you feel tension in your body? What sounds are louder than others?
See what you notice if your eyes are open or closed—if you are standing or sitting. Try different places inside your home, or pick a restful spot outdoors.

NEVER BE IN A HURRY;
DO EVERYTHING QUIETLY
AND IN A CALM SPIRIT.

Saint Francis de Sales

Breathe, intentionally.

In, 2, 3, 4... ——————— Out, 2, 3, 4...

Breathe in gently, fully

———————

Pause briefly between the inhale and exhale

———————

Slowly release your breath

AFFIRMATION
for embracing emotions

I CAN EXPERIENCE

EACH DAY AND SEE

WHAT FEELINGS COME

UP FOR ME WITHOUT

JUDGMENT.

MY EMOTIONS ARE

SAFE AND HELD.

Do not try to figure out how you shall feel or when you shall feel differently. Instead, trust. Accept today, but do not be limited by it... A new energy is coming. A new feeling is on the way. We cannot predict how it will be by looking at how it was or how it is, because it shall be entirely different.

MELODY BEATTIE

What is something you've held on to for possibly too long?

_____

_____

_____

What is something you wish you had a different perspective on?

_____

_____

_____

What do you wish you could begin again?

_____

_____

_____

How can you offer yourself some acceptance and peace with the above?

_____

_____

_____

With the new day
comes new strength
and new thoughts.

ELEANOR ROOSEVELT

Acknowledge your worries.

What is something that is top of mind for you today?

What is something you've been concerned about for a while?

Who is someone you can share these worries with who will support you?

MEDITATION:
Movement

Use walking, quickly or slowly, to be your guide. Notice the feel of each step, the tensing and releasing of muscles, and the sound your feet make as they are placed on the ground. If walking isn't possible or feeling right, try simply stretching or a few yoga movements. Feel the connection between your mind and your body, and enjoy the various sensations that come forward.

BE KIND TO YOUR
BODY, GENTLE WITH
YOUR MIND AND PATIENT
WITH YOUR HEART.

Becca Lee

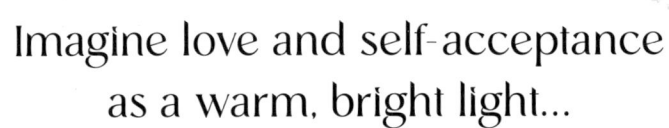

Imagine love and self-acceptance as a warm, bright light...

Feel the light come down from above

Feel the light fill the top of your head and move down through your chest

Feel the light expand into the rest of your body, down to the earth

Feel the light connect you to the ground, rooted and calm

How do you feel differently now
than you did a moment before?

AFFIRMATION
for trusting yourself

I LOOK WITHIN

WITH JOY AND

CURIOSITY.

I LET GO OF

DOUBT SO I MAY

LISTEN WHOLLY

TO MY HEART.

Find the love
you seek, by first
finding the love
within yourself.
Learn to rest in
that place within
you that is your
true home.

SRI SRI RAVI SHANKAR

What is one thing you want to offer your body today?

_____

_____

_____

What is one thing you want to offer your mind today?

_____

_____

_____

What is one thing you want to offer your spirit today?

_____

_____

_____

Caring for your own
body, mind, and spirit
is your greatest (and
grandest) responsibility.
It's about listening to the
needs of your soul and
then honoring them.

KRISTI LING

Get playful.

Which of these childhood activities sound most appealing?

- ○ Swinging
- ○ Coloring or doodling
- ○ Playing hide and seek
- ○ Daydreaming
- ○ Wearing a fun costume
- ○ Being barefoot
- ○ Telling silly jokes
- ○ Reading aloud
- ○ Singing
- ○ Climbing a tree
- ○ Asking lots and lots of questions
- ○ Talking with an imaginary friend
- ○ Playing a game or doing a puzzle
- ○ Blowing bubbles
- ○ Going for a bike ride
- ○ Collecting treasures
- ○ Seeing shapes in clouds

MEDITATION:
Visualization

Call on feelings of peace and relaxation with your mind. Bring forward any scene, goal, person, dream, or memory that holds great joy for you. Consider all five senses and add as much detail as possible. Who is nearby? What qualities do they possess? What are you wearing and what is the temperature? What emotions do you feel as you take it all in?

NURTURE YOUR MIND
WITH GREAT THOUGHTS...

Benjamin Disraeli

Let yourself *rest.*

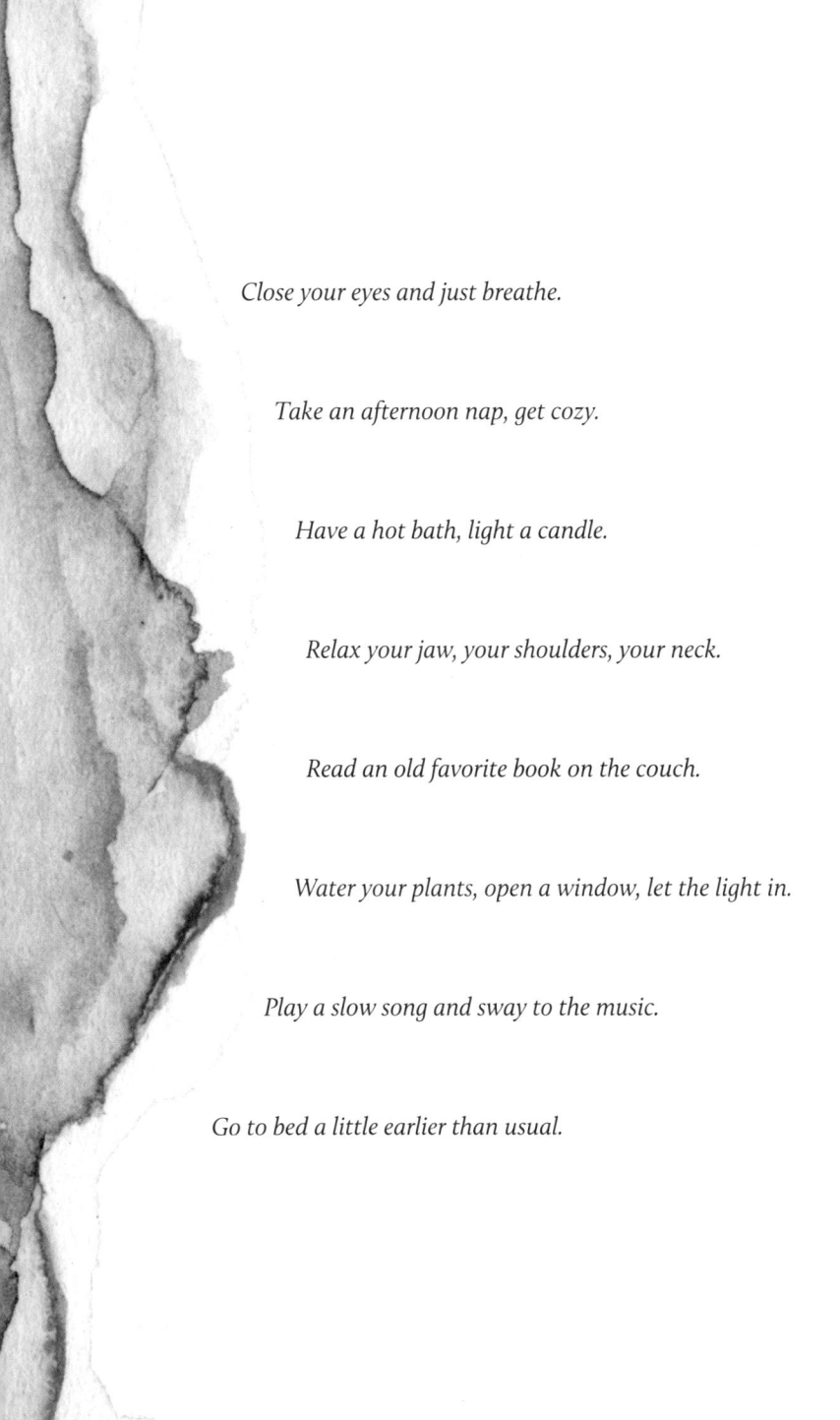

Close your eyes and just breathe.

Take an afternoon nap, get cozy.

Have a hot bath, light a candle.

Relax your jaw, your shoulders, your neck.

Read an old favorite book on the couch.

Water your plants, open a window, let the light in.

Play a slow song and sway to the music.

Go to bed a little earlier than usual.

AFFIRMATION
for restoring confidence

I TRUST IN MY OWN

INNER KNOWING.

MY POSSIBILITIES ARE

UNLIMITED AND

I EMBRACE ALL OF

MY POTENTIAL.

To accept
ourselves as
we are means
to value our
imperfections
as much as our
perfections.

SANDRA BIERIG

What is something you've always known deeply about yourself?

_____

_____

_____

_____

_____

_____

_____

What's something you do differently than most?

_____

_____

_____

_____

_____

_____

_____

Be faithful to
that which exists
within yourself.

ANDRÉ GIDE

Keep it simple.

What are a few of your favorite, simple things?

1.

2.

3.

MEDITATION:
Relaxation

Get yourself into some comfortable clothes and find a warm, quiet place to stand or lie down. Begin with the top of your head, consciously loosening every inch. Move down your body, slowly, intentionally relaxing each muscle. You may tighten gently to help cue your body to relax each part. If you find a spot that is wanting to keep the tension, don't worry. Just allow a few extra moments of focus: breathe into those places and offer yourself patience. It may take a few repetitions to allow your body to release all the tension.

...WITHIN YOU
THERE IS A STILLNESS
AND SANCTUARY
TO WHICH YOU CAN
RETREAT AT ANY TIME
AND BE YOURSELF...

Hermann Hesse

Wake up with
sweet thoughts.

Before you leave your bed in the morning,
take a few moments to think of the following...

Just one thing you're looking forward to in the upcoming day.

Just one thing that will make the day easier for you.

Just one thing that you love.

AFFIRMATION
for taking each day as it comes

I CAN FACE ALL

THAT COMES MY WAY.

I WILL RELY ON MY

STRENGTH, AND MY

JOY, TO EMBRACE

BOTH THE HIGHS AND

LOWS OF MY LIFE.

You don't always
need a plan.
Sometimes you
just need to
breathe, trust,
let go and see
what happens.

MANDY HALE

What is something you've always loved, all through the years?

What is something new and exciting that has come into your life?

What has been one of your most joyful experiences?

What is something beautiful you're looking forward to?

Your heart
knows your song,
but you have to
be willing to listen to
the words.

SUE ROCK

Create a day filled
with small joys.

A small joy to give yourself upon waking:

A small joy to give yourself in the morning:

A small joy to give yourself in the afternoon:

A small joy to give yourself in the evening:

A small joy to give yourself just before going to sleep:

MEDITATION:
Connection

Also called a "loving-kindness meditation," this practice is for both giving and receiving compassion. Sit quietly in a place that is comfortable for you. Start with yourself. Open your heart, think about all you are, and offer yourself a few messages of love and acceptance. Next, think about someone you love. Focus your feelings outward, toward them, and emotionally offer them kindness and gratitude. You may do this daily, thinking about a different person you care about each time. But don't forget to always begin with yourself.

ALL THE GREAT BLESSINGS
OF MY LIFE ARE PRESENT
IN MY THOUGHT TODAY.

Phoebe Cary

COMPENDIUM.
live inspired

Written by: Amelia Riedler
Designed by: Steve Potter
Edited by: Bailey Vega

ISBN: 978-1-957891-09-5

1st printing. Printed in China with soy inks on FSC®-Mix certified paper.

Create meaningful moments with gifts that inspire.

CONNECT WITH US
live-inspired.com | sayhello@compendiuminc.com

   @compendiumliveinspired
#compendiumliveinspired